COW

Written by
JULES OLDER

Illustrated by
LYN SEVERANCE

ini Charlesbridge

COW is dedicated to my favorite
Vermont farmer, Carroll Lawes.
He was born in 1914, died in 1987,
and raised cows in Brownington
the whole time.   —J. O.

COW is dedicated to my grandfather,
J. Herbert Severance, a sixth-
generation Vermont farmer who
had a fine herd of Guernseys.
                    —L. S.

Published by Charlesbridge Publishing
85 Main Street, Watertown, MA 02172-4411
(617) 926-0329

Printed in the United States of America
10 9 8 7 6 5 4 3 2 1

The illustrations in this
book were done in Dr. Ph.
Martin's Hydrus watercolors
on Strathmore Bristol stock.
The text type was set in Severance.
Color separations were made by Pure Imaging,
Watertown, Massachusetts.
Printed and bound by Worzalla Publishing
Company, Stevens Point, Wisconsin
This book was printed on recycled paper.
Production supervision by Brian G. Walker
Composition by Bill Harvey

Library of Congress Cataloging-in-
Publication Data
    Older, Jules.
    Cow/by Jules Older; illustrated by Lyn
Severance.
        p.   cm.
    Summary: A lighthearted, informative look at
cows: different breeds, what they eat, how they
make milk, and an assortment of other facts.
    ISBN 0-88106-957-4 (reinforced for library use)
    1. Dairy cattle—Miscellanea—Juvenile literature.
    2. Cows—Miscellanea—Juvenile literature.
    [1. Cows. 2. Dairy cattle.] I. Severance, Lyn, ill.
    II. Title.
    SF208.O58 1997
    636.2'142—dc20   96-947

Ben & Jerry's Ice Cream is pleased
to allow the use of "Severance"
type in support of a subject we
know & a person we love.

Jules and Lyn will both donate
7.5% of their profits from COW
to Heifer Project International,
which gives cows, goats, and lambs
to poor people all over the world.

TANKS A LOT
to the people who helped with this book.
Here they are: Ann Austin, Kent & Jeanette
Birch, Emily Carbonetti, Roger Clapp, Tom Gallagher, Stuart Gibson, Bill
Harvey, Jackson Harvey, Woody Jackson, Jerry Jerard, Sandy Keppler,
Sonya Kittredge, James Lawrence, Daria and Gabrielle MonDesire,
Juliana McIntyre, Don and Shirley Nelson, Anne Rauen, Kelly Swanson,
Sarah Swett, and Amber & Willow Older, Effin Older, Ruth & Y. T.
Older, Malka & D. J. Older (a lot of Olders, aren't there?)

FIRST

of all, this is a cow. Say "cow."
It rhymes with . . . Well it
rhymes with a lot of things:
pow and powwow; chow and
chow chow; bow and bowwow!

Cow also rhymes with *how*.
How do you learn about cows?
You start by turning the
page . . . *now!*

BOW-BWOW!?

SECOND,

where do cows live? Most cows live on farms. Cows spend a lot of their time—a *lot* of their time—munching grass in pastures.

In cold and snowy places, they move to barns in winter.

A lot of people in the North move to Florida in winter, but cows move to barns.

People in Florida eat oranges. Cows in barns eat grain. That's the way it goes.

COWS IN SUMMER

COWS IN WINTER

THIRD,

what do cows make that people like?

Cows make milk. Milk for calves, milk for kids, milk for grown-ups, milk for butter and for cheese, and, most important of all, milk for ice cream.

The reason cows can make milk is—and a lot of people get confused about this—because cows are female. Like mothers and sisters and Auntie Emma. Female. Cows are female cattle.

Male cattle are called *bulls.* Bulls can't make milk, but they're very good at snorting and pawing the ground. We won't talk much more about bulls because this book is about cows. That's why it's called *COW.*

FOURTH,

let's clear up one more thing: People talk about cows *giving* milk. Cows don't *give* milk. Cows *make* the milk, and either a calf or a farmer *takes* the milk.

They take it by pulling and squeezing on the cow's teats until the milk squirts out.

Calves do this pulling and squeezing with their mouth. Farmers do it with their hands or with milking machines. Calves take milk whenever they get thirsty. Farmers take milk two or three times a day, in the morning and in the evening and sometimes at night.

Now, do cows mind when the calf or the farmer takes their milk?

No, they don't mind.

Because if the calf or the farmer didn't take their milk, their udders, which in Vermont are called *bags,* would get so full they'd really hurt.

AM MILKING TIME PM

FIFTH,

how do cows make milk when all they eat is grass and hay and grain, and all they drink is water?

This is such a tough question that maybe we ought to think about it for a while.

For now, let's answer an easier one: When did cows first come to America?

The answer—and I'm not making this up—is May 14, 1611. That's nearly four hundred years ago.

In the early 1600s, the very first cow was brought to Jamestown, Virginia.

SIXTH,

let's talk about different kinds of cows. Dairy cows are the cows that make milk for butter and for cheese and, most important of all, for ice cream. You have your . . .
Holstein cows,
Guernsey cows,
Jersey cows,
Ayrshire cows,
Brown Swiss cows,
Dutch Belted cows,
and a lot of other kinds of cows.
Only you don't say "kinds of cows." You say *breeds* of cows.

HOLSTEIN

GUERNSEY

JERSEY

AYRSHIRE

BROWN SWISS

DUTCH BELTED

This is a Holstein. It's a big black-and-white cow that comes from the Netherlands. Or Germany. Nobody's quite sure.

This is a Guernsey. Guernseys come from an island in the English Channel, the Isle of Guernsey.

This is a Jersey. The first Jersey came from the island of Jersey, which is not in New Jersey. Jersey, the island, is another island in the English Channel. Jerseys are the smallest dairy cows.

This is an Ayrshire. It is a reddish-brown-and-white cow. Ayrshires come from Scotland.

This is a Brown Swiss. It's called a Brown Swiss because it is brown and it comes from Switzerland.

And this, believe it or not, is a Dutch Belted. (I'm not making this up. I'm not making any of this up.) You don't need to be a rocket scientist to see why it got its name.

There are also cowboys and cowgirls. And cowbirds and cowslips. And cowlicks. Here's a cowlick. The cowlick got its name because—can you guess? Right, because it looks like a cow licked it.

SEVENTH,

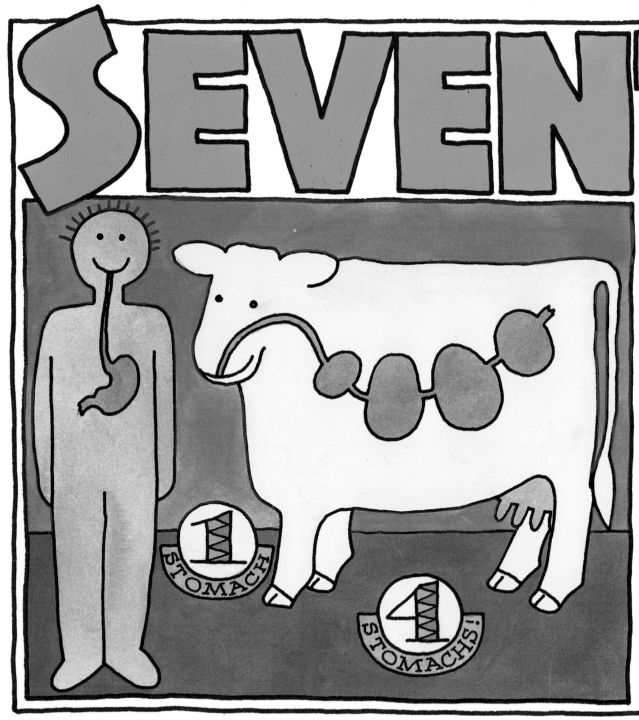

it's time to talk about how cows turn grass and hay and grain into milk. One part you may not believe, and another part may disgust you. But, remember, I'm not making any of this up.

A person—that's you—has only one stomach. How many stomachs do you think a cow has? (This is the hard-to-believe part.)

The correct answer is four.

That's right, a cow has four stomachs, and each stomach has a different name.

The first stomach is the *rumen*. Rumen rhymes with "two men." Tummy two is the *reticulum*. Reticulum rhymes with "Let's tickle 'em!"—more or less. The *omasum* ("Yo! Chase 'em!") is the cow's third stomach. And last, but not least, we have the *abomasum*, which doesn't rhyme with anything at all. Except "Yabbo race 'em," which doesn't mean anything at all.

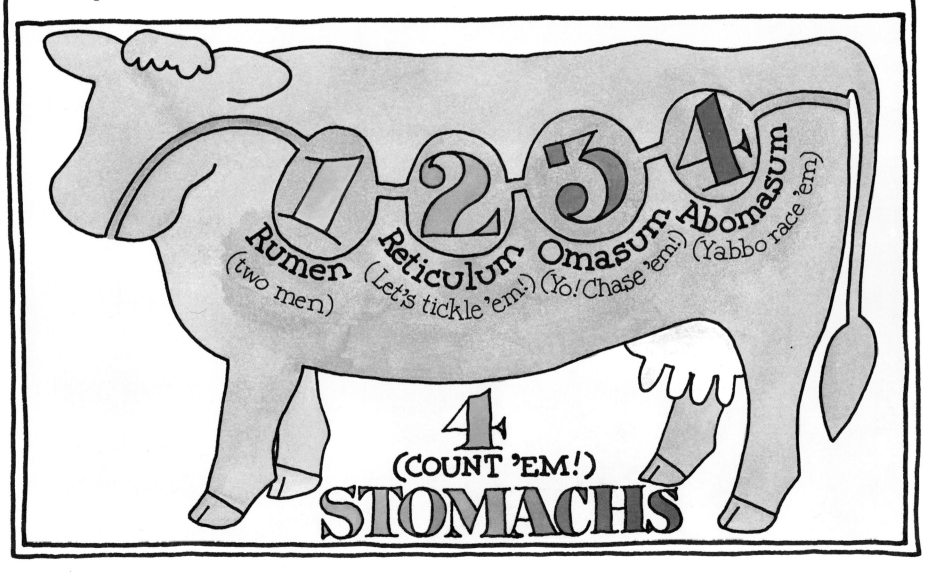

Those are the stomachs. Then there's the cud. That's the potentially disgusting part (P.D.P.).

Here's the cud story. The cow munches grass. The cow swallows grass.

(Don't try this at home.)

The grass goes down—actually *up* since the cow's mouth is down in the grass—the cow's long, long throat and into her rumen. Stomach number one, remember?

Going UP!

1 RUMEN

Inside the rumen, stomach juices, which are sort of like super spit, go to work on the grass, making it soft and gummy. Then the rumen sends it on to stomach number two, which is called— Anyone? Anyone?— which is called the reticulum,

2 RETICULUM

where it gets more of the juice treatment.

Then (and here comes the P.D.P.) the cow coughs up a ball of this half-digested food and chews it again!

This food ball is called *cud*. What the cow is doing is called *chewing the cud*.

Then, after a lot of lying and chewing and lying and chewing, the cow swallows what's left of the food for a *second* time. This time it goes to the third stomach,

P.D.P. ICK!

the omasum, and then on to the fourth, the abomasum. By  the time it gets through the abomasum, it is completely digested. Finally!

The good stuff in the grass goes into the cow's bloodstream and does all the usual things—makes bones, gives energy, builds strong muscles—and it also goes into her udder where it's turned into—ta da!—*m-i-l-k!*

That's what happens to the good stuff. What do you think happens to the leftover stuff?

It comes out the cow's rear end as urine and feces. Most people call cow feces *manure.*

Some people call cow feces *cow plops.* You can call them that, too. Say, "Cow plops."

And that's the story of how cows make milk. And cow plops. Which brings us to the . . .

EIGHTH,

and burning question, does chocolate milk come from brown cows?

C'mon, gimme a break!

Brown cows, black cows, red cows, and Dutch Belted cows all make white milk.

To make chocolate milk, add a tablespoon or two of cocoa or chocolate syrup to a glass of white milk.

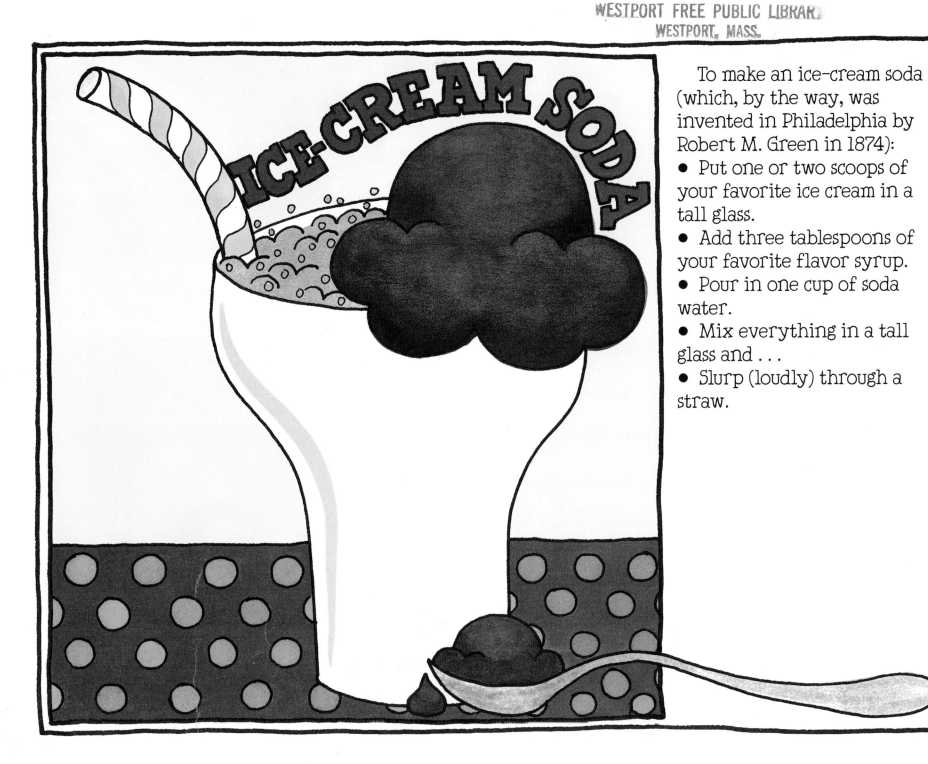

ICE-CREAM SODA

To make an ice-cream soda (which, by the way, was invented in Philadelphia by Robert M. Green in 1874):

• Put one or two scoops of your favorite ice cream in a tall glass.

• Add three tablespoons of your favorite flavor syrup.

• Pour in one cup of soda water.

• Mix everything in a tall glass and . . .

• Slurp (loudly) through a straw.

To make an ice-cream sundae (invented in Two Rivers, Wisconsin, in 1881 by Ed Berners):

• Take a scoop of ice cream and pour a couple of tablespoons of hot fudge on it.

• Then add another scoop of ice cream and pour four more tablespoons of hot fudge on it.

• Then add three tablespoons of whipped cream.

• Finally, sprinkle on a table-spoon of chopped walnuts and throw a cherry on top.

Here are two other facts about ice-cream sundaes that you can use to amaze your friends with your brilliance:

 The reason it's called a "sundae" instead of a "berners" is that Mr. Berners, who owned an ice-cream shop, made them on only one day of the week. The day was not Monday, not Tuesday, not Wednesday, not Thursday, not Friday, not Saturday—the day was S _ _ d _ _ y.

② Ice-cream sundaes made it into the *Guinness Book of World Records* in 1983. That's the year Ben & Jerry's created "the most monstrous ice-cream sundae ever concocted." That sundae stood almost twelve feet tall and weighed 27,102 pounds. They made it in a swimming pool!

No, I told you, I am not making any of this up!

Now, all that's left is to go to the . . .

S M T W Th F S

SUNDAY	MONDAY	TUESDAY	WEDNESDAY	THURSDAY	FRIDAY	SATURDAY
		1	2	3	4	5
6	7	8	9	10	11	12
13	14	15	16	17	18	19
20	21	22	23	24	25	26
27	28	29	30	31		

4 ft.   5 ft.   6 ft.

NINTH,

chapter and learn how a calf is born.

Like this.

If the calf is female, it's called a heifer (say "heffer"). If it's male, it's a bull calf (say "bull caff").

A heifer becomes a cow after she has a calf or two of her own.

But, we were talking about how a calf is born. Here are the true answers to the most important questions:

1. *Where* is the calf born? Usually in one of two places.

Farmers like cows to give birth in barns. They fix up a stall with a nice, soft sawdust floor so the cow will be clean and comfy—

and so the farmer can keep an eye on how the cow and her calf are getting along.

Cows like to give birth in the farthest corner of a pasture or behind a big bush or in a stand of trees. The truth is, they like to give birth in the hardest-to-get-to, hardest-to-find spot on the farm. Maybe they're shy.

2. What *part* of the calf is born first? Usually, nose first. Sometimes, legs first. Once in a while, *everything* first. When that happens, farmers have to help by reaching into the cow and turning the calf around.
3. What's the first thing a cow does *after* her calf is born? She licks it all over with her big, rough tongue.

4. What does the *calf* do? The calf sits awhile, then wobbles to its feet, then bunts around with its head until it finds its mother's teats. Then the calf has its first drink of milk.

The calf is happy.
The cow is happy.
The farmer is happy.

And *that* brings us to the . . .

TENTH,

chapter. It is filled with amazing cow facts that will convince your friends you are some kind of bovine genius.

1 There are around 1.3 billion cows in the world.

2 A cow produces between 60 and 200 pounds of milk a day.

3 The average cow produces 100 pounds of manure a day.

PEE-YEW!

4 She drinks 15 to 30 gallons of water a day.

5 She eats about 50 pounds of food a day.

6 Cows are big. They weigh from 800 to nearly 2,000 pounds. Don't let a cow step on your foot unless you want a severe case of fallen arches.

7 Cows are curious. If a stranger walks into the pasture, all the cows come over to have a look.

CALF YOU COW

9 Cows are peaceful creatures, *but* if you get between a cow and her calf, watch out, mister! Some cows also kick you with their hooves and swat you with their long tails, which have been lying in cow plops all day long.

8 Cows like music. A lot of farmers keep a radio on in the barn to make the cows happy.

10 A cow can make milk when she's two years old and has had her first calf.

AND THAT'S THE STORY OF COWS & THE END of COW MOoo

THE END

A QUIZ,

QUESTIONS **ANSWERS**

?

Questions

FINALLY
(AND THIS TIME I
REALLY MEAN IT),
here's a bovine quiz.

1. Are cows born with horns?

2. Are bulls born with horns?

3. Do cows grow horns, or is it just bulls?

4. Then how come you see so many cows without horns?

5. How do calves know who their mother is?

6. Who is the world's best-known cow?

7. Who was the world's most destructive cow?

8. What's the difference between beef cows and milking cows?

9. Can you milk a beef cow?

10. Are some breeds better at eating grass than others?

Answers

1. Nope.

2. Also, nope.

3. Both of them do.

4. Because farmers de-horn them. And some are bred as polled animals. *Polled* means they never grow horns.

5. They can tell by the smell.

6. It's a toss-up. Since the 1930s, the Borden Company has used Elsie as its trademark. (Elsie has a husband, Elmer, and a daughter, Beulah.) But in 1972, a Vermont artist named Woody Jackson started painting black-and-white cows all over the place, and pretty soon the Woody Jackson cow became famous, too. By the way, Woody's cow is named Rubin's Cow. Why not Woody's Cow I hear you ask? Because Woody named it after his dog, a golden retriever called Rubin.

7. We don't know her real name, but everybody calls her Mrs. O'Leary's cow. In 1871, while Mrs. O'Leary was milking her, she kicked over a kerosene lamp and set the hay on fire, which set the barn on fire, which set the house on fire, which set the block on fire, which set *Chicago* on fire!

8. Beef cows put their energy into muscle, not milk, so they grow up with smaller udders and bigger bodies.

9. It depends on the breed. The Devon and the Shorthorn, yes. They're dual-purpose breeds. But Herefords and Anguses are too skittish for most farmers to milk, and they don't give much milk anyway.

10. Yes. Jerseys and Brown Swiss are good grazing cows. When they're in the pasture they do more eating than Holsteins, who tend to do a lot of lying around and loafing.

gift
10-15-97